BEULAH has a HUNCH!

Inside the Colorful Mind of Master Inventor Beulah Louise Henry

Katie Mazeika

Beach Lane Books

New York London Toronto Sydney New Delhi

Beulah Louise Henry was frustrated.
Again.

Scritch . . .
　　　scratch . . . erase!

Beulah had a hunch, a new idea for an invention. She could see it clearly in her mind, and she desperately wanted to draw it in perfect detail. But no matter how precise the image in her head was, the drawing on her slate was a mess.

Mr. Henry was frustrated too. Lying on the floor to draw was not ladylike, and the chalk dust covering Beulah's frock was unseemly. Mrs. Henry was beside herself. What would the neighbors think? A nine-year-old was expected to behave better than this! They sent Beulah to clean up before she was to join them outside.

At the end of each day, the family sat on the porch and greeted the neighbors who stopped to chat on their strolls. Beulah tried to sit and smile politely, as her mother did, with her ankles crossed and her hands in her lap.

But the birds in the yard called to her with their colorful songs and the mysterious intricacies of their nests. All around her there were things to explore and figure out.

Beulah's parents called her a daydreamer. But she wasn't daydreaming. Beulah was always exploring and searching for problems, such as household items that didn't work as well as they could. When she spotted a problem, her mind would fixate, working on a solution until—Aha! She had a hunch.

That's what she called the inventions that appeared in her mind. Beulah's brain worked differently from most other people's. She had hyperphantasia, an ability to picture things in extreme detail. Beulah could think about a problem and, eventually, visualize the solution fully formed, with gears whirring and wheels spinning.

When Beulah drew a hunch, she was trying to copy the detailed image in her mind so other people could understand it.

Beulah wanted to understand what made the things around her work. To her parents' dismay, Beulah took apart her mother's mantel clock and looked for clues in the springs and gears. She wasn't impressed by the clock's fancy façade. She wanted to understand how it knew when to chime.

Beulah examined the newfangled gas range. But she wasn't interested in learning how to cook or bake. She wanted to know how the buttons and knobs turned the heat on and how they made the flame grow higher.

Beulah couldn't find the answers in her lessons.

She was taught poetry and music, etiquette and elocution.

She learned sewing, dancing, and all the things a young lady was expected to know. That meant no science or math allowed.

But Beulah didn't want to become a proper society lady; she wanted to be an inventor. So Beulah did the only thing she could: she kept seeking out problems and sketching her hunches. As she did, she focused on making each drawing cleaner and each detail clearer.

Beulah saw more than hunches. She also had synesthesia. She called it "color-hearing." So for Beulah, every time she heard a number, she saw a particular color, and every name had a hue.

Whenever she listened to music, she saw a color for each note. Rainbows gamboled around her on the dance floor as she learned to waltz.

One evening as Beulah stayed on the porch with her parents, she noticed that ladies walking by often carried parasols in the hot North Carolina sunshine, along with vanity cases that held calling cards, coins, and cosmetics.

Beulah had a hunch!

What if she could make a compartment in the parasol handle to hold calling cards and other small items, eliminating one thing that ladies had to carry?

Now that Beulah was thinking about parasols, she had another hunch! To make parasols smaller, she could create a collapsible handle, like a telescope. But parasols weren't just practical—they were fashionable, too. Stylish ladies liked to match their parasols to each outfit.

And Beulah had a hunch for that!

What if she could make a parasol even more versatile, with interchangeable fabric covers in different colors?

retracts!
compact
to carry

hinges
like a door

must
detach!

SPRINGS
like a
sofa!

Ladies could swap them out so one
parasol could match several outfits,
instead of having to buy a new parasol
for each occasion. Beulah knew her
hunches would help people save money
and space—and be stylish, too!

Beulah rushed to find a pen and capture her hunches on paper. She figured out the compartment and collapsible handle right away, but the interchangeable covers posed some issues. How could Beulah attach the fabric cover to the parasol? The covers needed to be swapped out easily yet hold up to the strongest winds.

For weeks the problem simmered in Beulah's brain until at last she saw the solution in full three-dimensional detail.

Beulah was confident that women across the country would clamor for her parasol. But before she could produce it, she needed a patent for her invention. A patent would prove that the parasols were her idea, and no one else could copy them. But patents required intricate technical drawings—more intricate than any drawing Beulah knew how to make. So she took her drawings to a local draftsman, William Woodley.

Together the two of them worked tirelessly for weeks. Beulah redrew and reexplained her vision again and again until William had precisely illustrated each angle. At last Beulah's hunch was on the page, and perfect.

Beulah sent in her application, detailing the telescoping handle, the integrated coin purse, and the interchangeable fabric, and after more than two years of waiting, she got her patent!

Now all Beulah had to do was find someone to produce her parasols. But local manufacturers just shook their heads and shooed her away.

"Ladies belong in the home, NOT in business!"

Beulah refused to be discouraged.

She traveled all the way to New York City. Some manufacturers laughed at the idea of a woman inventor. Several others just shrugged her off. One manufacturer told Beulah she was wrong, that a parasol with interchangeable covers couldn't be made.

Beulah knew it was possible, and she was
going to prove it. She borrowed a hammer and
a nail and set out to make a prototype herself.

First she made a hole through
a steel rib of her parasol.

Then with a nail file
she carved a snap out of
a bar of soap.

The snap passed through the hole and
attached the fabric to the steel rib. It worked,
proving that her hunch was possible.

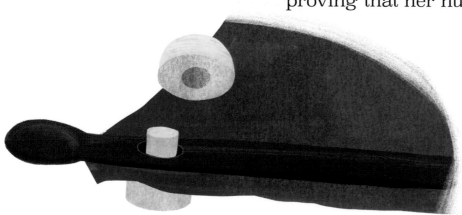

The next day, confident with her patent and handmade prototype, Beulah set out to meet with one last manufacturer. This one said yes. They would produce Beulah's parasol!

Less than a year later, the front windows of America's first and fanciest department store, Lord & Taylor, were filled with color, showcasing Beulah's parasols.

Each mannequin was dressed to match a parasol cover. The window display reminded Beulah of music, each note a different hue. Beulah stood on the sidewalk, proudly admiring the colorful array of Snappon Umbrellas—her hunch come to life.

Women everywhere bought the parasols, just like Beulah had known they would. Beulah was officially a successful inventor. She took the money she made from her parasols and bought two manufacturers of her own: one to continue making her umbrellas and one to produce her many other hunches.

Beulah handpicked a team of draftsmen, mechanics, and model makers. They interpreted her drawings and detailed descriptions and helped her bring her hunches to life.

Beulah kept seeing problems to solve all around her. Soap that sank to the bottom of the bathtub?

Beulah had a hunch!

Dolly Dips, sponges cut into doll shapes that floated and were filled with soap.

Teddy bears too stiff to cuddle?

Beulah had a hunch!

She invented stuffed animals with bendable limbs and filled with soft cotton batting instead of sawdust.

Beulah had hunches for many more toys after that, like a rubber doll that kids could bathe, and a doll with eyes that closed and changed color. When she saw new dolls on the market that said "Mama," she had a hunch and created a doll that said "Mama" and "Papa."

Toys weren't the only things Beulah invented. She had hunches for everything from ice cream makers to factory machinery. By her fortieth birthday she held more patents than any other woman in history. The patent office started to call her "Lady Edison," after the famous inventor Thomas Edison. The press loved the nickname, and they loved Beulah.

She opened the doors of her New York City hotel suite and gave interviews to women's magazines and scientific publications. Beulah charmed the reporters. She offered them southern biscuits hot from a grill invention that popped out of a hole in the wall, and she served them tea on a table she'd made that collapsed and rolled under the bed.

Scritch . . . scratch . . . erase!

For the rest of her life, Beulah still drew most of her hunches while lying on the floor, not caring if she got her dress dirty, surrounded by her pet birds, tortoises, and Chickadee the cat, with the lights and sounds of Times Square in the background, and color dancing all around her.

More on Beulah Louise Henry

By the end of her life, Beulah Henry held forty-nine known patents just through her own companies. What is a patent? If someone invents a new product or technology, they can apply to the government for a patent. If their patent is granted, it gives that person an exclusive right to the product or process for a set number of years—which means no direct competition. Although the exact number of Beulah's inventions is unknown, experts credit her with more than one hundred inventions. Despite her lack of technical education, she made innovations in factory machinery for her own companies as well as other manufacturers. To this day she holds the record for the most mechanical patents granted to a woman.

Beulah was born in Charlotte, North Carolina, in 1887. Public education was still a relatively new idea, and there was just one public elementary school in all of Charlotte, a fast-growing Southern city. Because Beulah came from a prominent family (she was a descendent of American founding father Patrick Henry), she attended a small private girls' school and then a finishing school. In these schools, girls were taught to be proper ladies and homemakers. At the time, many people believed that women couldn't learn complex math or science, so those subjects were left to the boys while the girls prepared to be wives and mothers—and nothing more. The girls took classes in art, literature, foreign languages, music, manners, and morality. They attended dances, recitals, and teas. Any basic math taught was only what a woman would need to run a home. Science courses were limited to hygiene, basic anatomy, and first aid.

Despite her lack of math and science education, from a young age Beulah was determined to figure out how things worked, and to invent better products. Beulah found ways to work around her lack of math and science education. As an adult she built a technical team that understood her layman's terms and sketches and helped her bring invention after invention to life. Beulah developed such a reputation as an inventor and problem-solver that other manufacturers would come to her with their problems, and she would find solutions and develop designs for them.

Beulah was also an astute businesswoman. She sold forty thousand Snappon Umbrellas in just two months! Beulah used that money to set up a company to continue creating and improving her umbrellas, called Henry Umbrella and Parasol Co. Inc., and a second company, B. L. Henry Company, to develop her other inventions. Beulah also strategically decided to patent her inventions around the world, not just in the United States. Most countries have their own patent offices and laws, and by patenting her designs in other countries, she practically guaranteed that she would be the only producer of her inventions worldwide.

Beulah often spoke about what she called her "color-hearing." She described seeing color when she heard music, and associating specific colors with certain names, numbers, and musical notes. The official term is synesthesia, and it can include all five senses—some people associate certain smells or tastes with sounds or sights. And like with most neurodiverse conditions, there is a spectrum of synesthesia. Some people with the condition are aware of it but unbothered; for others it can lead to sensory overload and make specific environments unbearable.

Beulah also had hyperphantasia, which is the ability to see things in the mind's eye as clearly and vividly as in reality, with every single detail. Beulah saw her hunches, products, and inventions fully formed and functioning in her mind. She pictured things in three dimensions, where she could rotate an object around and look at it from any angle, and shrink or enlarge any part without losing clarity or detail. There is also a spectrum for hyperphantasia; few people have it to the extent that Beulah had. At the other end of the spectrum, some people have aphantasia, which means they can't visualize anything in their mind. Most people are somewhere in between. While hyperphantasia is common among inventors, it doesn't mean the inventions appear like magic in the person's mind. When Beulah saw a problem, she would think about it for as long as it took until—Aha! She had a hunch. Once Beulah had an idea, her hyperphantasia would then allow her to see the solution perfectly formed in her mind's eye.

Beulah's impact on everyday items can be seen today. A version of the collapsible umbrella handle, which was part of Beulah's famous Snappon Umbrella invention, is still used in modern umbrellas. The dolls Beulah invented in the 1900s were the basis for many of today's dolls that blink, cry, and speak. And several of the sewing machine and typewriter innovations Beulah patented have been further developed and are still part of contemporary machines.

But what is even more significant is Beulah's lasting impact on women in STEM. She was featured in magazines for women, in magazines for scientists, and in local newspapers. The spotlight on Beulah proved that a woman could be a world-class inventor, and that a woman could thrive in an industry dominated by men. Beulah also advocated for neurodiversity well before the term had been coined. She spoke openly about her "hunches" and her synesthesia, and in doing so she showed that neurodiversity wasn't something to stigmatize but to celebrate.

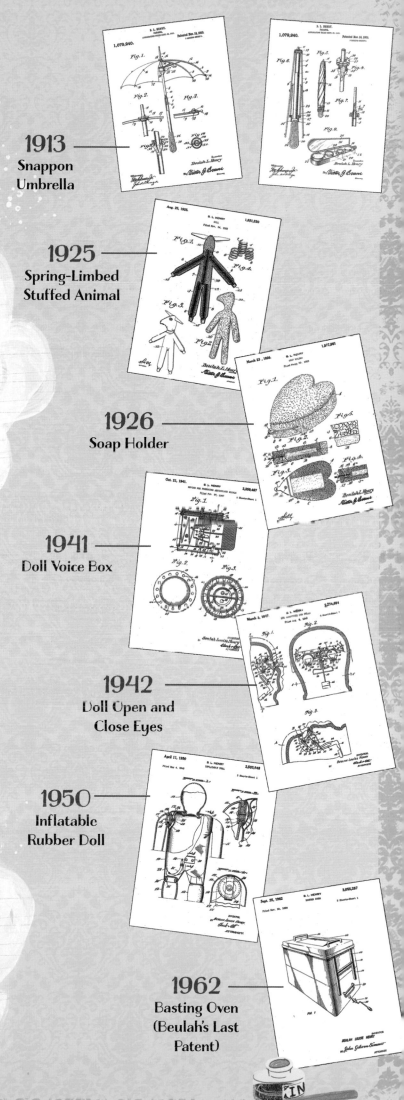

1913
Snappon Umbrella

1925
Spring-Limbed Stuffed Animal

1926
Soap Holder

1941
Doll Voice Box

1942
Doll Open and Close Eyes

1950
Inflatable Rubber Doll

1962
Basting Oven (Beulah's Last Patent)

To my husband, Chris, my best friend
and rock. Thank you for being there
from the beginning, cheering me on.

SOURCES

Callahan, Rosellen. "What the Spirits Said in Lady Edison's Laboratory." *News Tribune* (Tacoma, WA), August 21, 1938.

Camp, Carole Ann. *American Women Inventors* (Collective Biographies). Berkeley Heights, NJ: Enslow Publishers, 2004, 35–42.

Dick, Gerry. "Woman Invents Varied Gadgets." *Public Opinion* (Chambersburg, PA), April 7, 1937.

"Lady Edison": Woman Inventor with Fifty-Two Patents Ascribes Success to "Inner Vision." *Literary Digest*, May 8, 1937.

Leatherdale, Lyndsay. *Synesthesia. The Fascinating World of Blended Senses: Synesthesia and Types of Synesthesia Explained*. Ashford, England: IMB Publishing, 2013.

Macdonald, Anne L. *Feminine Ingenuity: How Women Inventors Changed America*. New York: Ballantine Books, 1992, 395–411.

Parton, Mary Field. "Your Girl Makes Good." *McCall's*, November 1930.

"She Can Make Anything with Scissors and a Hairpin." *News and Observer* (Raleigh, NC), August 10, 1924.

Stanley, Autumn. *Mothers and Daughters of Invention: Notes for a Revised History of Technology*. New Brunswick, NJ: Rutgers University Press, 1995, 420–6.

BEACH LANE BOOKS • An imprint of Simon & Schuster Children's Publishing Division • 1230 Avenue of the Americas, New York, New York 10020 • © 2023 by Katie Mazeika • Book design by Rebecca Syracuse © 2023 by Simon & Schuster, Inc. • All rights reserved, including the right of reproduction in whole or in part in any form. • BEACH LANE BOOKS and colophon are trademarks of Simon & Schuster, Inc. • For information about special discounts for bulk purchases, please contact Simon & Schuster Special Sales at 1-866-506-1949 or business@simonandschuster.com. • The Simon & Schuster Speakers Bureau can bring authors to your live event. For more information or to book an event, contact the Simon & Schuster Speakers Bureau at 1-866-248-3049 or visit our website at www.simonspeakers.com. • The text for this book was set in Charcuterie Flared. • The illustrations for this book were rendered digitally. • Manufactured in China • 0623 SCP • First Edition • 10 9 8 7 6 5 4 3 2 1 • Library of Congress Cataloging-in-Publication Data. • Names: Mazeika, Katie, author. • Title: Beulah has a hunch! : inside the colorful mind of master inventor Beulah Louise Henry / Katie Mazeika. • Description: First edition. | New York : Beach Lane Books, [2023] | Includes bibliographical references. | Audience: Ages 4-8 | Audience: Grades 2-3 | Summary: "Meet Beulah Louise Henry, a girl with a knack for problem-solving who grew up to be a world-famous inventor, in this captivating picture book biography. When Beulah Louise Henry spotted a problem, she fixated on it until, AHA! She had a hunch. That's what Beulah called the inventions she came up with to solve the problems she saw all around her. Beulah's brain worked differently. She had hyperphantasia, which meant she saw things in extreme detail in her mind, as well as synesthesia, which caused words and numbers and even music notes to show up as different colors in her brain. Beulah's unique way of seeing the world helped her think up vivid solutions to problems—her hunches were fully formed with gears whirring and wheels spinning. When Beulah grew up, she had a hunch for a new & improved parasol. She worked on a patent and prototype, and her parasol became a huge success! From there, Beulah went on to invent everything from cuddly stuffed animals to ice cream makers to factory machinery, earning the nickname 'Lady Edison.' And it all started with a hunch!"—Provided by publisher. • Identifiers: LCCN 2022046871 (print) | LCCN 2022046872 (ebook) | ISBN 9781665903639 (hardcover) | ISBN 9781665903646 (ebook) • Subjects: LCSH: Henry, Beulah Louise, 1887–1973. | Women inventors—United States—Biography—Juvenile literature. • Classification: LCC T40.H39 M39 2023 (print) | LCC T40.H39 (ebook) | DDC 609.2 [B]—dc23/eng/20221201 • LC record available at https://lccn.loc.gov/2022046871 • LC ebook record available at https://lccn.loc.gov/2022046872